Traditional German Cooking Made Easy with Authentic German Recipes

A Taste of Germany

Sarah Spencer

All rights reserved © 2020 by Sarah Spencer and The Cookbook Publisher. No part of this publication or the information in it may be quoted from or reproduced in any form by means such as printing, scanning, photocopying, or otherwise without prior written permission of the copyright holder.

This book is presented solely for motivational and informational purposes. The author and the publisher do not hold any responsibility for errors, omissions, or contrary interpretation of the subject matter herein. The recipes provided in this book are for informational purposes only and are not intended to provide dietary advice. A medical practitioner should be consulted before making any changes in diet. Additionally, recipes' cooking times may require adjustment depending on age and quality of appliances. Readers are strongly urged to take all precautions to ensure ingredients are fully cooked in order to avoid the dangers of foodborne illnesses.

ISBN: 9798614667559
Printed in the United States

THE
COOKBOOK
PUBLISHER

www.thecookbookpublisher.com

CONTENTS

INTRODUCTION	1
BEEF DISHES	5
PORK DISHES	17
CHICKEN DISHES	27
SEAFOOD DISHES	37
SIDE DISHES	45
SOUPS	61
BREADS	73
DESSERTS	87
RECIPE INDEX	111
APPENDIX	113

INTRODUCTION

Germany is famous for its lush, green beauty, its deep forests, and its ancient cities and castles. The country has plains, forests, mountains, rivers, and seas, and as a result, regional foods vary significantly, but because of the short growing season, they do tend to center around meats, dairy, grains, and potatoes. These foods are filling and delicious and made with the care and dedication to quality that is ingrained in German culture.

Join us on a gastronomic tour of this unique country, where we'll show you how to make authentic Pork Schnitzel, soft and chewy Pretzels, and your own homemade Sauerkraut. But you'll also find some delicious recipes for foods that are less well-known, like Beef Rouladen (a tasty rolled beef with mustard and onion) and Potato Dumplings.

Meals in Germany tend to be hearty, and food features prominently in the many celebrations and festivals in the country, including Christmas and Oktoberfest – an autumn celebration that lasts for two weeks and dates back to the early 1800s, when the Crown Prince of Bavaria, Ludwig, married the Princess Therese of Saxon-Hildburghausen. The people were invited to join in the celebration, and it has been carried out almost every year since.

Oktoberfest highlights the foods Germany is famous for – sausages and beer – and it's a party that has spread all over the world, where many different versions of "German" cuisine have developed. In many cases, these celebratory foods are not technically German in origin, but we love them all the same. However, this book shares only authentic German recipes. We love to celebrate culture through food, and we wanted to share with you what the German people really eat.

Because Europe is small, there are some influences from nearby countries like France, Hungary, and Austria, but the Germans have developed their own versions. For example, German Gulasch is rich with a broth made of simmered onions, and Germany's answer to Cordon Bleu is a delight.

Bread is a true staple in Germany, and traditionally, it would be served fresh with a meal. If you love to bake, take some time to try making your own using the recipes in this book. Bierocks are a bun stuffed with meat, and they're an underrated lunchbox favorite!

Another thing you're going to love about German food is dessert! German bakers might go a little overboard at Christmas, but who doesn't love Pfefferneuse? And do be sure to try our favorite, Plum Custard Kuchen.

Coffee and Cake

Germany has a lovely tradition of pausing every afternoon to sit down and have coffee, cake, and conversation. Accordingly, the country has a rich selection of cakes and biscuits, and we've shared some of the best ones with you here. Set some time aside for yourself to indulge in some Franzbötchen (German style cinnamon rolls), or chat with some friends over Bienenstich (Bee Sting Cake). Of course, we'll also show you how to make other traditional favorites as well!

BEEF

Beef Rouladen

These tasty beef rolls are a satisfying change to your usual weekday supper lineup. They take only a few minutes to put together, and are rich with the flavors of mustard, onion, and bacon.

Serves 8 | Prep. time 15 min. | Cooking time 40 min.

Ingredients
8 (4-ounce) pieces round steak, pounded to ¼-inch thick
¼ cup Dijon mustard
½ cup minced onion
2 cloves garlic
2 teaspoons salt
1 ½ teaspoons paprika
1 teaspoon freshly ground black pepper

8 slices bacon
½ cup all-purpose flour
2 tablespoons butter
1 (12-ounce) can beef broth
2 cups water, divided
2 tablespoons cornstarch
¼ cup sour cream

Directions
1. Lay out the steaks and spread them each with half a tablespoon of mustard. Sprinkle on the onion and garlic and season each with salt, paprika, and pepper.
2. Lay one slice of bacon on each and roll them up individually, like jelly rolls. Pierce the rolls with toothpicks to secure them, and dredge them in the flour.
3. Heat a large skillet over medium-high heat and melt the butter. Brown the rolls on all sides.
4. Add the beef broth and 1 cup of water to the skillet. Cover, reduce the heat, and simmer until the rolls are cooked through, about 30 minutes.
5. Remove the rolls to a plate and keep them warm.
6. Strain the cooking broth back into the skillet.
7. Combine the cornstarch with the remaining cup of water and add it to the skillet. Cook, stirring often, until it thickens. Mix in the sour cream.
8. Serve the rouladen with a generous serving of the gravy.

Sauerbraten

Sauerbraten is a meat dish that is marinated in a combination of vinegar and wine. Traditionally, it can be made with mutton, venison, horse, pork, or beef. (We'll use beef.)
The acidity is nicely offset with the addition of a very unique ingredient!

Serves 6–8 | Prep. time 20 min. | Marinating time 4 days | Cooking time 5 hours

Ingredients
4 pounds beef round rump roast
2 onions, thinly sliced
10 peppercorns
3 whole cloves
1 bay leaf
1 cup white vinegar
1 cup red wine
½ cup water
¼ cup vegetable oil

1 teaspoon salt
2 cups boiling water
12 gingersnaps, crushed
½ cup sour cream
1 tablespoon all-purpose flour

Directions

1. Place the roast in a glass or ceramic bowl. Add the onions, peppercorns, cloves, and bay leaf.
2. Combine the vinegar, wine, and water and pour the mixture over the meat.
3. Cover the bowl and keep it in the fridge for 4 days, turning the meat twice each day.
4. Strain the marinade, reserving the onions and one cup of liquid. Dry the meat with paper towels.
5. Heat the oil in a Dutch oven. Season the roast with salt and brown it on all sides. Add the onions.
6. Pour the boiling water into the pot and add the gingersnaps. Cover and simmer for 1 ½ hours, turning the meat from time to time.
7. Add the reserved marinade and cook for another 2–3 hours, until tender.
8. Transfer the meat to a cutting board, cover it with foil, and let it rest.
9. Strain the cooking liquid and add it back to the pot. Combine the sour cream with the flour and stir the mixture into the broth. Stir and cook until it is thick and bubbly.
10. Slice the meat and add it back to the gravy.

False Hare (Falscher Hase)

From the name, you might not guess that this dish is a German version of meatloaf, baked with eggs inside. The name came about after WWII, when meat was scarce. What could be found was ground and shaped into a meatloaf that was roughly the shape of a hare, which was a favorite in Germany.

Serves 6–8 | Prep. time 20 min. | Cooking time 45 min.

Ingredients
1 (4-inch) piece of baguette, or 4 slices white bread
2 tablespoons butter
1 small white onion
2 pounds lean ground beef
2 eggs
2 teaspoons paprika
1 teaspoon dried thyme
¼ teaspoon ground nutmeg

¼ cup fresh parsley, chopped
1 tablespoon salt
4 hard-boiled eggs
¼ cup breadcrumbs
1–2 cups water

Directions
1. Place the baguette or bread in a bowl and soak it with water. Set the dish aside.
2. Melt the butter in a skillet and cook the onions until they are translucent, about 5 minutes. Let them cool.
3. Preheat the oven to 425°F and butter a roasting pan.
4. In a mixing bowl, combine the ground beef with the eggs (the raw ones), paprika, thyme, nutmeg, parsley, and salt. Add the cooked onion. Squeeze the water out of the baguette or bread and add the bread to the mixture. Blend well.
5. Divide the meat in two. Shape half of it into a long oval, about 5x12 inches.
6. Roll the boiled eggs in the breadcrumbs and arrange them in a row on the meat.
7. Form another oval with the remaining meat and lay it on top of the eggs.
8. Shape the mixture into a loaf and transfer it to the prepared baking dish.
9. Bake the meatloaf for about 45 minutes, or until it reaches 165°F internally. From time to time, add half an inch of water to the baking pan. This will help prevent the meatloaf from burning.

Meat Patties (Frikadellen)

Frikadellen originated in the north of Germany, near Hamburg, and eventually gave rise to our beloved hamburger. These are more carefully seasoned than your average burger, and are eaten both hot and cold, often with potato salad.

Serves 6–8 | Prep. time 15 min. | Chill time 30 min. | Cooking time 10 min.

Ingredients
4 slices white bread, torn
½ cup warm milk
5 tablespoons olive oil, divided
1 large yellow onion, minced
3 cloves garlic, minced
1 pound ground beef (80%, not lean)

12 ounces ground pork
2 large eggs
½ cup chopped fresh parsley
2 teaspoons salt
1 ½ teaspoon ground black pepper
2 teaspoon prepared yellow mustard
2 teaspoons dried marjoram
1 teaspoon sweet Hungarian paprika
1 teaspoon ground ginger
½ teaspoon ground mace
½ teaspoon ground coriander
⅛ teaspoon ground cardamom
2 tablespoon butter

Directions
1. Place the bread in a large bowl and pour the milk over it. Let it sit for a few minutes.
2. Meanwhile, heat 1 tablespoon of oil in a skillet over medium heat and cook the onions until they take on a nice golden color. Add the garlic and cook for 1–2 more minutes.
3. Add the cooked onion mixture, beef, pork, eggs, and seasonings to the bowl with the bread and milk. Mix well and knead for a few minutes.
4. Form the mixture into patties the size you want. Chill for at least 30 minutes.
5. Heat a large skillet over medium-high heat, and add the remaining oil and the butter. Fry the patties until they are golden on both sides and are cooked through (to a temperature of 165°F.)

German Gulasch

This is Germany's version of Hungarian Gulasch, traditionally made with as much onion as meat. The cooked onion forms the basis of the delicious sauce. This is a great meal for a chilly day – the scent fills the house and brings hungry bellies to the table. If you plan ahead, you can soak up the sauce with some warm Potato Bread.

Serves 6 | Prep. time 15 min. | Cooking time 2 ½ hours

Ingredients
¼ cup butter
2 pounds yellow onions, finely chopped
2 pounds trimmed beef chuck, cut in 1 ½-inch cubes
4 cloves garlic, chopped
1 teaspoon caraway seeds
1 teaspoon dried oregano
2 tablespoons sweet paprika
2 tablespoons tomato paste

2 tablespoons red wine vinegar
1 ½ cups beef broth
1 bay leaf
1 teaspoon kosher salt
½ teaspoon ground black pepper

Directions
1. Preheat the oven to 325°F.
2. In a Dutch oven on the stovetop, melt the butter over medium heat and slowly cook the onions until golden, about 30 minutes.
3. Add the remaining ingredients (do not brown the beef). Bring the mixture to a simmer and transfer it to the oven. (You can cook it on the stovetop if you prefer.)
4. Bake, covered, for 2 hours. Stir it occasionally throughout, and leave the lid off for a while if it needs to thicken.
5. Remove the bay leaf, check and correct the seasonings, and serve hot.

Cabbage Rolls with Gravy (Kohlrouladen)

We're used to seeing cabbage rolls in tomato sauce, but many German family recipes use beef gravy instead. We highly recommend you try it with a side of creamy mashed potatoes.

Serves 4 | Prep. time 30 min. | Cook time 45 min.

Ingredients
For the kohlrouladen
1 head of cabbage (large leaves only)
1 pound ground beef
1 medium onion, diced
1 teaspoon salt
½ teaspoon black pepper
½ teaspoon garlic powder
½ teaspoon ground ginger
⅛ teaspoon ground cloves

For the sauce
1 can beef broth
1 cup water
1 small onion, diced
2 bay leaves
2 cloves garlic, minced
1 tablespoon cornstarch

4 cups mashed potatoes, for serving

Directions
1. Place the cabbage in a large pot and add enough water to cover. Bring it to a boil and then lower the heat. Simmer, turning the cabbage often, until you can peel off the outer large leaves without tearing them. Repeat until you have enough large leaves to work with (10–12).
2. Preheat the oven to 350°F and butter a baking dish.
3. In a mixing bowl, combine the beef, onion, and spices for the filling.
4. Spoon a portion of the beef filling onto a cabbage leaf and roll, tucking in the sides. If your leaves are very thin, you may choose to add another layer. Secure the roll with a toothpick and place the cabbage roll in the baking dish. Repeat until you have used all the filling.
5. Combine the sauce ingredients and pour them over the rolls. Cover the baking pan with foil and bake for 45 minutes, or until the internal temperature of the meat filling reaches 165°F.
6. Remove the bay leaves. Serve the rolls with a spoonful of the gravy and a side of mashed potatoes.

PORK

Pork Schnitzel

German schnitzel (Schweineschnitzel) is made with pork, as opposed to the Austrian version, Weinerschnitzel, which is made with veal. These delicious cutlets are often accompanied by a side of Spaetzle. You can serve them plain with a splash of lemon and parsley, as shown, or with a thick mushroom sauce (and then you would call it Jäegerschnitzel.)

Serves 4 | Prep. time 15 min. | Cooking time 15 min.

Ingredients
4 boneless pork chops
1 ½ teaspoons salt, divided
½ teaspoon freshly ground black pepper
½ cup all-purpose flour
2 eggs

1 cup plain breadcrumbs
Canola oil for frying

Mushroom gravy
2 tablespoons bacon grease (or butter)
1 yellow onion, finely chopped
2 cloves garlic, minced
1 pound fresh mushrooms, cleaned and sliced
¼ cup butter
¼ cup all-purpose flour
2 cups condensed beef broth
Dash balsamic vinegar
½ teaspoon dried thyme
Salt and pepper to taste

Directions
1. Start by preparing the gravy, if using. (If not, skip to step 7.)
2. In a skillet, melt the bacon grease over medium-high heat. Add the onion and cook until golden.
3. Add the garlic and cook 1–2 more minutes.
4. Add the mushrooms and cook for 6–8 minutes, stirring occasionally, until they are browned and the liquid has evaporated.
5. Add the butter and sprinkle on the flour, stirring to coat everything. Let it cook another minute or two.
6. Add the broth, vinegar, thyme, and a generous amount of salt and pepper. Cover and let it simmer on low while you cook the pork, stirring occasionally.
7. One at a time, place the pork chops between 2 pieces of plastic wrap and pound them to a thickness of ¼ inch. Season them on both sides, using 1 teaspoon of salt and the black pepper.
8. Arrange a dipping station. In one bowl, combine the flour with the remaining salt. In a second bowl, beat the eggs. Place the breadcrumbs in a third bowl.
9. Heat the oil to 335°F. It should be deep enough to immerse the meat.

10. Dip the pork to coat both sides and the edges in flour, egg, and then breadcrumbs. Do not press the breadcrumbs onto the meat.
11. Immediately after coating the chops, slide them into the oil. Cook for 2–3 minutes on each side, until golden.

Bratwurst

If you don't have a meat grinder but you want to try making sausages from scratch, you can buy the meats pre-ground. A sausage stuffer is strongly recommended, but you can create sausage patties if you don't have one Serve these with some homemade Sauerkraut!

Serves 8–12 | Prep. time 30 min | Chill time 30 min. | Cooking time 30 min.

Ingredients
1 ¼ pounds pork butt, ground
1 pound veal or beef, ground

½ pound pork fatback, ground
1 tablespoon kosher salt
1 ½ teaspoons ground black pepper
1 ½ teaspoons red pepper flakes
1 teaspoon dried marjoram
½ teaspoon caraway seed
½ teaspoon grated nutmeg
½ teaspoon ground ginger
¼ teaspoon ground allspice
¼ teaspoon ground ginger
5 feet of natural sausage casing

For the beer bath
6 cups German lager or ale
1 cup butter
2 large onions, thinly sliced
2 cloves garlic, chopped
1 teaspoon red pepper flakes
1 bay leaf
Salt and pepper to taste

Directions
1. If you're grinding the meat, trim and chill it first and then grind it with a 3/16-inch plate.
2. Combine the meat with the spices and chill for 30 minutes.
3. Stuff the sausages according to the sausage-stuffer directions and twist it into 4-inch links. Separate the sausages if you like.
4. Refrigerate the brats, but use them within a day or two.
5. Prepare the beer bath by combining the ingredients in a large skillet or Dutch oven. Bring it to a low simmer.
6. Grill the sausages over medium heat until browned.
7. Immerse the sausages in the hot bath and let them sit for 15–20 minutes.

Currywurst

Currywurst is German street food – a sausage served with a curried ketchup mixture and served (often on a narrow paper plate) with more curry powder on top.

Serves 4–6 | Prep. time 10 min. | Cooking time 30 min.

Ingredients
6 sausages, such as bratwurst
1 tablespoon butter
1 cup tomato ketchup, divided
¾ cup water
¼ teaspoon baking soda
2 teaspoons onion powder
¼ teaspoon cayenne powder
½ teaspoon black pepper
2 tablespoons Worcestershire sauce
2 tablespoons curry powder

Directions
1. Lay the sausages on a cutting board and slash diagonal cuts in them on both sides, just piercing the casing and a little of the filling, but not cutting all the way through.
2. Melt the butter in a skillet over medium heat and fry the sausages until they are brown and crisp. (You can grill them if you prefer.)
3. Remove the sausages from the skillet and keep them warm.
4. Into the skillet, pour the ketchup, water, and baking soda. Stir while the mixture fizzes; this is reducing the acidity.
5. Stir in the seasonings and the Worcestershire sauce and let is simmer a minute or two.
6. Serve the sauce over the sausages with a sprinkle of curry powder on top.

Maultaschen

Similar to ravioli, maultaschen is a kind of meat dumpling from Swabia, an area in the southwest of Germany. As with ravioli, the choices for fillings are many. Our recipe is made with ground pork.

Serves 4 | Prep. time 30 min. | Rest time 20 min | Cooking time 10–13 min.

Ingredients
2 cups all-purpose flour
2 eggs, lightly beaten
2 tablespoons olive oil
3 tablespoons water
⅔ cup frozen spinach, thawed and drained
1 onion, chopped
8 ounces ground pork
1 tablespoon Worcestershire sauce
3 tablespoons breadcrumbs
1 teaspoon salt
½ teaspoon black pepper
¼ teaspoon ground nutmeg

For the egg wash
1 egg, beaten
2 tablespoons milk

Directions
1. Prepare the dough by combining the flour, eggs, olive oil, and water. Mix until the dough comes together and knead until smooth. Let it sit at room temperature, covered with a clean, damp towel, for 20 minutes.
2. In a blender, combine the spinach, onion, pork, Worcestershire sauce, breadcrumbs, salt, pepper, and nutmeg.
3. Prepare the egg wash.
4. Roll half the dough thinly into a rectangle and paint it with a layer of egg wash.
5. Spoon teaspoons of the filling onto the surface in rows, leaving room to form the edges of the dumplings.
6. Make a matching rectangle with the other piece of dough and brush it with egg. Lay it on top of the fillings, egg side down.

7. With your fingertips, gently press the layers together, paying special attention to the spaces between the filling.
8. With a pizza cutter or knife, separate the dumplings. Seal the edges with a fork.
9. Boil 6 cups of water, and simmer the dumplings for 10–13 minutes.

Bratwurst Supper

This is one easy weeknight way to serve bratwurst. It's a one-pot meal complete with vegetables.

Serves 4 | Prep. time 30 min. | Cooking time 30 min.

Ingredients
¼ cup butter
2 pounds bratwurst sausages

2 pounds small red potatoes
1 large yellow onion
½ cup red and green bell peppers, diced
8 ounces mushrooms, sliced
Salt and pepper to taste

Directions
1. In a large skillet over medium heat, melt the butter. Slice and add the sausages, and cook until they begin to brown.
2. Add the potatoes and cook another 5 minutes, stirring occasionally.
3. Add the onion, peppers, and mushrooms and cook until they are done to your liking.
4. Season with salt and pepper, and serve.

CHICKEN

German Chicken Fricassee

You can make this fricassee with leftovers, and it's just as good as when you have time to simmer a whole chicken.

Serves 8–12 | Prep. time 30 min. | Chill time 30 min. | Cooking time 30 min.

Ingredients
¼ cup butter, divided
8 ounces fresh mushrooms, sliced
1 ½ pounds boneless skinless chicken, cubed
¼ cup all-purpose flour
2 cups chicken broth

1 teaspoon dried thyme
½ teaspoon red pepper flakes
1 cup frozen mixed vegetables (or use leftovers)
½ cup heavy cream
Salt and pepper to taste

Directions
1. Melt half the butter in a hot skillet and cook the mushrooms until browned.
2. Add the remaining butter and the chicken pieces. Cook until they are lightly browned.
3. Sprinkle the flour over the chicken and mushrooms and stir to coat.
4. Pour in the chicken broth, thyme, and red pepper flakes. Bring it to a boil, stirring occasionally. Cover and simmer for 15–20 minutes.
5. Add the vegetables and cream. Season with salt and pepper and cook to heat through.

Oktoberfest Roast Chicken (Weisn Hendle)

Yes, we love sausages at Oktoberfest, but don't forget the delicious roast chicken! Keep in mind that in Germany, roast chickens tend to be quite small. You might choose to prepare a few.

Serves 6 | Prep. time 15 min. | Cooking time 1 hour

Ingredients
2 whole chickens, about 3 pounds each
1 tablespoon salt
1 tablespoon sweet paprika
½ teaspoon dried thyme
½ teaspoon dried oregano
½ teaspoon ground pepper
½ teaspoon dried marjoram
½ teaspoon ground rosemary

¼ cup butter, sliced

Directions
1. Preheat the oven to 325°F and butter a baking pan large enough to hold the chickens.
2. Pat the chickens dry with paper towels.
3. In a bowl, combine all the spices and mix well.
4. Rub the chickens (inside and out) with the spice mixture and set them in the baking pan.
5. Pour half an inch of water in the baking pan. Arrange the butter slices on top of the chickens.
6. Bake for about an hour, or until the meat reaches 175°F in the thickest part of the thigh. Baste from time to time. Let them rest, covered, for 15 minutes before serving.

Beer Grilled Chicken

Combine the flavors of beer, mustard, and lemon in this delicious barbecued chicken.

Serves 6 | Prep. time 15 min. | Cooking time 30 min.

Ingredients
½ cup peanut oil
2 teaspoons grainy German mustard
1 cup dark German beer
¼ cup lemon juice
3 cloves garlic, minced
1 teaspoon salt
1 teaspoon black pepper
1 teaspoon dried basil
½ teaspoon dried rosemary
4 pounds bone-in chicken pieces

Directions

1. In a large bowl or resealable bag, combine the oil, mustard, beer, lemon juice, garlic, salt, pepper, basil, and rosemary.
2. Add the chicken pieces and turn to coat. Cover or seal, and refrigerate for at least 2 hours, preferably overnight.
3. Preheat the grill over medium heat and oil the grates.
4. Remove the chicken pieces from the marinade and place them on the grill; discard the marinade.
5. Cook until the skin is crisp, turning the pieces to brown them all over. Reduce the heat, cover the grill, and cook until the chicken is cooked through.
6. Serve with a good German mustard and your choice of sides.

Drunken Chicken in Red Wine (Beschwipster Huhn)

This chicken simmered in a light wine broth is tender and flavorful.

Serves 6–8 | Prep. time 15 min. | Cooking time 1 hour

Ingredients
6–8 chicken pieces
1 teaspoon salt
½ cup all-purpose flour
6 slices bacon, diced
2 tablespoons butter
2 onions, chopped
4 carrots, sliced
4 stalks celery, sliced
3 cloves garlic, chopped
1 ½ cups chicken broth
2 ½ cups red wine

1 sprig fresh rosemary
5 sprigs fresh thyme
1 bay leaf
Mashed or roasted potatoes for serving

Directions
1. Season the chicken with salt and coat it with the flour. Set it aside.
2. In a Dutch oven, cook the bacon until crisp. Remove the bacon pieces from the pot, but leave the grease.
3. Brown the chicken pieces in the bacon fat and remove them to a platter.
4. Leaving all the browned bits, melt the butter in the pot and add the onion, carrots, and celery. Cook until softened, and then add the garlic. Cook another minute or two.
5. Add the broth, wine, rosemary, thyme, and bay leaf. Transfer the chicken pieces back to the pot.
6. Cover and simmer for 45 minutes, until the chicken is cooked through and tender.
7. Remove the rosemary and thyme stems and the bay leaf, and serve the chicken pieces with the broth.

Black Forest Chicken Cordon Bleu

Germany and France are close neighbors. Try the German version of this classic dish, made with Black Forest ham and Limburger cheese.

Serves 4 | Prep. time 15 min. | Cooking time 30 min.

Ingredients
4 boneless skinless chicken breasts
½ teaspoon paprika
1 teaspoon garlic powder
½ teaspoon salt
½ teaspoon black pepper
8 slices German Black Forest ham
4 ounces German Limburger cheese, sliced, rind removed
1 ½ cups all-purpose flour
3 eggs, beaten

1 ½ cups breadcrumbs
Olive oil cooking spray

Directions
1. Preheat the oven to 375°F and coat a baking dish with cooking spray.
2. Butterfly the chicken breasts and season them with paprika, garlic powder, salt, and pepper on both sides.
3. On each piece of chicken, layer two slices of ham and one ounce of the cheese. Fold the breasts closed and secure the edges with a toothpick or two.
4. Arrange a dipping station with the flour in one bowl, the eggs in another, and the breadcrumbs in a third.
5. Dredge the chicken in the flour, egg, and then breadcrumbs. (Repeat the coatings if desired.)
6. Arrange them in the baking pan and spray them with olive oil cooking spray.
7. Bake for 30 minutes, or until they are 175°F internally.

FISH AND SEAFOOD

Fish Burgers (Fischbrötchen)

You find these delicious fish sandwiches served at food trucks and fast food places in northern Germany.

Serves 4 | Prep. time 5 min. | Chill time 1 hour | Cooking time 10 min.

Ingredients
4 (4-ounce) filets herring, mackerel, or salmon
1 tablespoon butter
Salt and pepper to taste
4 whole grain burger buns, sliced
Lettuce
4 thick tomato slices
4 thick slices dill pickle
8 thin slices red onion

Remoulade sauce
½ cup mayonnaise
1 hardboiled egg, finely chopped
3 gherkin or cornichon pickles
1 tablespoon fresh parsley, chopped
½ teaspoon dried dill weed
2 tablespoons minced sweet onion
1 tablespoon pickle juice
Salt and pepper to taste

Directions
1. Prepare the remoulade sauce by combining all the ingredients. Refrigerate for an hour, and then taste and adjust the seasonings to your liking.
2. Place a skillet over medium heat and melt the butter.
3. Season the fish with salt and pepper and cook it on both sides until it is lightly browned and flakes easily with a fork.
4. Toast the buns, if desired.
5. To assemble the sandwiches, spread a generous amount of the remoulade on all the slices of bun (tops and bottoms). Layer on some lettuce, tomato, pickle, red onion, and fish, and finish with the top of the bun.
6. Serve warm.

Cod in Mustard Cream Sauce

This fish dish is delicately flavored and pairs beautifully with a side of potatoes. You can customize the amount of mustard to suit your preference.

Serves 4–6 | Prep. time 15 min. | Cooking time 30 min.

Ingredients
1 ½ pounds cod fillets
2 tablespoons lemon juice
1 quart water
¼ cup chopped parsley, stems separate
6 whole peppercorns
1 bay leaf
1 onion, chopped
2 tablespoons Dijon mustard
½ cup heavy cream
1 teaspoon dill weed
6 tablespoons butter
Salt and pepper to taste

Directions
1. Sprinkle the fish fillets with the lemon juice and set them aside.
2. Pour the water into a large saucepan and add the parsley stems, peppercorns, bay leaf, and onion. Bring the mixture to a boil and cook for 20 minutes.
3. Cut the fish into serving pieces and place them in the water. Reduce the heat and simmer about 10 minutes, until the fish flakes easily.
4. Remove the fish to a plate and keep it covered.
5. Strain the cooking liquid and add 1–2 cups back to the pot. Add the remaining chopped parsley, the mustard, cream, dill, and butter. Cook over medium heat to reduce it a little, and season with salt and pepper (or more mustard) to taste.

6. Serve the fish with the sauce.

Marinated Fried Herring

This fish dish also hails from the north of Germany, which is natural, considering that the southern parts of the country are landlocked.

Serves 4 | Prep. time 30 min. | Rest time 24 hours | Cooking time 15 min.

Ingredients
4 fresh herrings, cleaned
1 teaspoon salt
½ teaspoon black pepper
2 tablespoons flour
3 tablespoons butter or oil for frying
1 cup red wine vinegar
1 cup vegetable broth
1 bay leaf
2 whole cloves
10 black peppercorns

1 tablespoon mustard seeds
1 (8-ounce) jar mixed pickles drained
1 (8-ounce) jar cocktail onions, drained
3 hot chilies, halved

Directions
1. Lay the fish flat and press to break the bones along the spine. Season them with salt and pepper and coat them with flour.
2. In a large skillet, heat the butter or oil. Add the fish and fry them until they are golden brown. Set them aside to cool.
3. Meanwhile, in a saucepan, combine the red wine vinegar, vegetable broth, bay leaf, cloves, peppercorns, and mustard seeds. Bring the mixture to a boil, reduce the heat, and simmer for 5 minutes. Remove it from the heat and let it cool.
4. Place the fish in a bowl and add the pickles, onions, and chilies. Pour the simmered liquid over, cover, and refrigerate for at least 24 hours (and up to a few days) before serving.

German Beer Fish (Bier Fisch)

This is an old German dish usually made with carp, but you can use a more available variety if you like.

Serves 4 | Prep. time 10 min. | Cooking time 35 min.

Ingredients
2 pounds whole carp, heads removed
2 tablespoons butter
1 onion, diced
1 stalk celery, diced
6 whole peppercorns
1 teaspoon salt
2 whole cloves
1 bay leaf
1 small lemon, sliced
10 ounces beer
6 gingersnap cookies, crushed
1 tablespoon sugar

Directions
1. Lay the fish flat and press to break the bones along the spine.
2. In a large skillet, melt the butter. Add the onion, celery, peppercorns, salt, cloves, bay leaf, and lemon slices and arrange them on the bottom of the pan.
3. Place the fish on the lemons and pour in the beer.
4. Cover the skillet and simmer for 15–20 minutes, until the fish is cooked through.
5. Strain the cooking liquid and add 1 ½ cups back to the skillet. Add the crushed cookies and the sugar. Cook and stir until it thickens, and remove the bay leaf
6. Serve the fish with the sauce.

SIDES

Traditional German Potato Salad

The main difference between traditional German potato salad and the creamy kind you might be more used to is that in authentic German recipes we tend to cook the sauce ahead of time, there's no mayo, and we include savory ingredients like beef broth.

Serves 8–10 | Prep. time 15 min. | Chill time 30 min. | Cooking time 20 min.

Ingredients
4 pounds Yukon Gold potatoes
8 ounces bacon, chopped
1 large white onion, finely diced
½ cup cider vinegar
3 tablespoons sugar
1 tablespoon kosher salt
2 cups beef broth
½ cup chopped fresh parsley

Directions
1. Peel the potatoes and simmer them in salted water until tender. Drain and let them cool.
2. Meanwhile, cook the bacon in a skillet until crisp, and then remove it from the pan with a slotted spoon. Set the bacon aside.
3. In the hot bacon fat, cook the onions until browned. Stir in the vinegar, sugar, and salt, and bring the mixture to a simmer.
4. Carefully slice the hot potatoes into a heatproof bowl. Pour the hot onion mixture over the potatoes and toss them to coat.
5. Heat the broth in the skillet and simmer to reduce it by half. Pour it over the potatoes. Stir gently.
6. Top with the chopped bacon and parsley. Serve immediately.

Spaetzle

This popular side dish makes a great alternative to rice, potato, or dry pasta – and it's surprisingly easy to make!

Serves 6 | Prep. time 5 min. | Cooking time 7 min.

Ingredients
1 cup all-purpose flour
¼ teaspoon ground nutmeg
½ teaspoon salt
1 pinch black pepper
2 eggs
¼ cup milk
2 tablespoons butter (or bacon fat)
3 tablespoons chopped fresh parsley
Salt and pepper to taste

Directions
1. In a mixing bowl, combine the flour, nutmeg, salt, and pepper.
2. In a separate bowl, beat the eggs. Add them to the flour alternately with the milk. Mix until a smooth dough forms.
3. Press the dough through the larger holes in a strainer.
4. Boil water sufficient to cook the noodles, about 8 cups.
5. Add the spaetzle in small batches and boil 5–7 minutes.
6. Meanwhile, melt the butter or bacon fat in a skillet. Fry the cooked spaetzle until they take on some nice color, and serve with a sprinkle of parsley and salt and pepper to taste.

Sauerkraut

Yes, you can buy sauerkraut, but it's easy and very inexpensive to make at home. Naturally fermented foods are very good for you, containing lots of healthy vitamins and nutrients as well as lactobacillus bacteria, which are great for your gut.

Makes 6 cups | Prep. time 30 min. | Fermenting time 1–3 weeks

Ingredients
1 head cabbage (about 4 ½ pounds)
2 tablespoons pickling salt (or another iodine-free salt)

Directions
1. Clean and dry a 6-cup mason jar.
2. Quarter the cabbage and remove the core. Thinly slice the cabbage and place it in a large mixing bowl.

3. Sprinkle on the salt, and with clean hands, knead, turn, and mix the cabbage with the salt. You want to bruise the cabbage to encourage the juices to come out.
4. When you have enough liquid to immerse the cabbage, transfer the mixture to the mason jar. Use a muddler or wooden spoon to press the cabbage down under the brine.
5. Cover the surface of the liquid with a piece of plastic wrap and put in a weight to keep the cabbage from floating up. (A small ramekin works well.)
6. Cover the top of the jar with cheesecloth and place the jar in a cool, dark place, like a cupboard.
7. If any mold should develop on the glass above the surface, just wipe it away with a cloth. The cabbage inside the brine will not be affected.
8. Check the sauerkraut after a week, but you can let it ferment for up to 3 weeks. When you're satisfied with the flavor, cover the jar with a lid and transfer it to the fridge.

Potato Pancakes (Kartoffelpuffer)

We might call them reibekuchen, rievekooche, or hash brown patties, but these German treats are delicious no matter what we say. Typically, they are served with apple sauce, but everyone has their favorite way to enjoy them.

Serves 6 | Prep. time 15 min. | Cooking time 20 min.

Ingredients
6 medium potatoes, washed or peeled
1 small onion
2 eggs
2 tablespoons all-purpose flour
¼ teaspoon baking powder
1 teaspoon salt
½ teaspoon pepper
Oil for frying

Apple sauce, for serving

Directions
1. Grate the potatoes and onion and transfer them to the middle of a clean kitchen towel. Fold the towel around the vegetables and twist to squeeze out as much liquid as you can. Transfer the potato and onion to a bowl.
2. Add the other ingredients and mix well.
3. Heat a thin layer of oil in a large skillet over medium-high heat.
4. Scoop out a spoonful of the potato mixture and gently flatten it in the pan. Cook on both sides until browned. Repeat until all the mixture is used.

Potato Dumplings (Kartoffelkloesse)

These dumplings are tasty comfort food at its best. They're fun and easy to make, and your family will enjoy the change.

Serves 8 | Prep. time 15 min. | Cooking time 1 hour

Ingredients
2 large russet potatoes
2 eggs, lightly beaten
¼ teaspoon cayenne pepper
¼ teaspoon ground nutmeg
Salt and freshly ground black pepper to taste
1 cup all-purpose flour
1 tablespoon minced fresh chives

For the bread filling
1 stick unsalted butter
2 cups fresh bread cubes

Directions
1. Heat the oven to 400°F and roast the potatoes until they are tender, about 40 minutes. Let them cool enough to handle.
2. While the potatoes cook, prepare the filling. Melt the butter in a skillet over medium heat. Add the bread cubes and cook, stirring often, until the bread is crispy and browned. Remove the bread from the skillet with a slotted spoon, leaving the browned butter in the pan.
3. Peel the potatoes and place them in a large mixing bowl. Stir in the eggs, cayenne pepper, nutmeg, salt, and pepper.
4. Add the flour and mix just to combine.
5. Scoop out a spoonful of the potato mixture about the size of a golf ball. Form it into a ball and press your thumb into the middle. Fill the indent with a spoonful of bread cubes (2 or 3 cubes), and shape the potato around the filling. Repeat until all the potato mixture is used. (There may be bread cubes left, which will be used for topping.)
6. Boil a large pot of water. Lower the dumplings one at a time into the boiling water with a slotted spoon. Cook for 1–2 minutes, until they float to the top.
7. Lower the heat, cover the pot, and simmer for 15–20 minutes. Turn the dumplings after 10 minutes.
8. Arrange the dumplings on a platter. If you like, you can drizzle them with browned butter and crumble the remaining bread cubes on top. Season with salt and pepper and top with chopped chives.

Onion Pie (Zwiebelkuchen)

Zwiebelkuchen is a dish often served in the autumn, when the air is crisp and cool. It makes a good breakfast, lunch, or supper.

Serves 6 | Prep. time 20 min. | Cooking time 1 hour

Ingredients
1 recipe pastry for a 9-inch single crust pie
3 pounds onions, sliced
3 slices bacon
1 cup sour cream
2 eggs
1 tablespoon all-purpose flour
½ teaspoon salt
½ teaspoon caraway seed

Directions
1. Heat the oven to 425°F and arrange the pastry in the pie plate, making sure it covers the sides. Trim the edges.
2. Sauté the onion in a large skillet until it is translucent. Transfer it to a heatproof bowl.
3. Cook the bacon, drain it, and chop it up. Add it to the onions and mix well.
4. Stir in the sour cream.
5. Beat the eggs lightly with the flour and salt, and stir them into the onion mixture.
6. Spread the filling in the pie crust and sprinkle on the caraway seed.
7. Bake for 1 hour, or until the onions are golden.

Red Cabbage

One of the hallmarks of German cuisine is the combination of sweet and sour, showcased in this colorful recipe for a popular side dish. It's often referred to as *Rotkohl* or *Blaukraut*, and is even better left over.

Serves 4 | Prep. time 10 min. | Cooking time 1 hour

Ingredients
3 tablespoons butter
1 large onion, thinly sliced

1 medium head red cabbage, shredded
3 apples, peeled and shredded
1 cup water
3 tablespoons cider vinegar
1 tablespoon sugar
1 ½ teaspoons salt
½ teaspoon ground black pepper
½ teaspoon ground nutmeg
¼ teaspoon ground cloves
2 tablespoons lemon juice
2 tablespoons cornstarch

Directions
1. In a Dutch oven or large pot, melt the butter and sauté the onion until it begins to soften.
2. Add the cabbage and apples and cook, stirring often, for 5–10 minutes, until it all begins to wilt.
3. Add the water, vinegar, sugar, salt, pepper, nutmeg, and cloves. Mix well.
4. Cover and let it simmer for 45 minutes to an hour, until the cabbage is soft.
5. Combine the cornstarch with the lemon juice and add it to the mixture. Taste and add more seasonings if desired. Cook, uncovered, until it thickens a little.

German Pancake (Pfannkuchen)

The "Dutch Baby," the baked pancake that resembles a Yorkshire pudding, is an American invention. This is a German family recipe for something that is more like a crepe, only thicker. Hint: use real buttermilk. You won't be sorry!

Serves 4 | Prep. time 10 min. | Cooking time 10 min.

Ingredients
4 eggs
2 tablespoons sugar
¼ teaspoon salt
1 cup all-purpose flour
1 cup whole milk
1 cup buttermilk

¼ cup butter for frying
Options for serving: fruit, berries, syrup

Directions
1. In a mixing bowl, whisk the eggs. Add the sugar, salt, and flour, and mix briefly before slowly adding the milk and buttermilk.
2. Heat a skillet over medium-high heat. Melt a generous amount of butter and pour in batter to make the size pancake you want.
3. Cook until the pancake is bubby and golden around the edges, and then flip it and cook it on the other side.
4. Repeat (with a fresh pat of butter) until all the batter is cooked. To serve, you can roll, stack, or fold them in fours. Enjoy!

SOUPS

Oxtail Soup

The marrow from the oxtail bones gives this soup its rich and hearty broth, and it's sure to hit the spot on a cold winter afternoon.

Serves 6–8 | Prep. time 20 min. | Chill time 12 hours | Cooking time 5 hours

Ingredients
1 pound oxtail, cut into 2-inch thick slices
3 tablespoons oil
4 garlic cloves, halved
¾ cup red wine
8 cups water
1 teaspoon salt
½ teaspoon black pepper

2 carrots, peeled and diced
2 parsnips, peeled and diced
1 large onion, diced
3 stalks celery, diced
2 medium potatoes, peeled and diced
1 teaspoon dried thyme
1 teaspoon dried parsley

Directions
1. The day before making the soup, heat a large pot over medium heat. Warm the oil and brown the oxtail pieces on all sides.
2. Add the garlic and cook for 1–2 minutes, and then pour in the wine, water, salt, and pepper.
3. Lower the heat and simmer for 3 hours. Remove the oxtail pieces from the broth. Cool and refrigerate them overnight in separate containers.
4. The next day, skim any fat from the broth and place the broth in a large soup pot. (It will have gelled, but it will liquify as it heats.)
5. Meanwhile, remove any obvious fat on the meat and separate the meat from the bones. Add the meat to the soup.
6. Add the vegetables and herbs to the pot, adding a little more water or wine to cover them if necessary. Bring the pot to a boil and simmer on low for 2 hours.
7. Check the seasonings and serve.

Midnight Soup
(Mitternachtssuppe)

If you like taco soup, you'll love this. Germany's version is traditionally served on New Year's Eve.

Serves 8 | Prep. time 15 min. | Cooking time 40 min.

Ingredients
2 tablespoons olive oil
1 ½ pounds lean ground beef
1 large onion
2 cups multicolored bell peppers, chopped
3 cloves garlic, minced
1 tablespoon chili powder
1 teaspoon paprika (sweet, hot, or smoked are all good)
1 teaspoon salt
1 teaspoon sugar
½ teaspoon dried oregano
½ teaspoon black pepper
1 (14-ounce) can red kidney beans
1 (6-ounce) can tomato paste
6 cups water
1 cup red wine
¼ cup heavy cream (or to taste)

Directions
1. Heat the oil in a Dutch oven over medium heat.
2. Add the beef and cook until it is browned, crumbling it with the spoon as you go. Drain any excess fat.
3. Add the onion, peppers, and garlic. Cook, stirring occasionally, until the vegetables begin to soften. Season with chili powder, paprika, salt, sugar, oregano, and pepper. Mix well and cook another minute or two.
4. Add the kidney beans, tomato paste, water, and wine. Bring the mixture to a boil, reduce the heat, and simmer 20–30 minutes on low.
5. Stir in the cream just before serving.

Lentil and Pork Shank Stew

This hearty stew comes from Berlin. The smoky flavor from the pork is the perfect balance for the earthy lentils. Try this with a slice of crusty bread and butter.

Serves 8 | Prep. time 10 min. | Cooking time 40 min.

Ingredients
2 tablespoons butter
1 carrot, diced
1 parsnip, diced
1 onion, diced
2 stalks celery, diced
1 leek, diced (white parts only)
2 cloves garlic, chopped
1 pound brown lentils
2 smoked pork shanks, cooked
2 quarts chicken or vegetable stock
Fresh thyme and chopped parsley

Salt and pepper to taste

Directions
1. Melt the butter in a Dutch oven and add all the vegetables. Cook until they begin to sweat and soften.
2. Meanwhile, sort and rinse the lentils. Add them to the pot.
3. Add the pork shanks and the broth. Bring the soup to a boil, lower the heat, and simmer about 30 minutes, or until the lentils are cooked to your liking.
4. Add the thyme and parsley and season with salt and pepper to taste.

Onion Soup (Zwiebelsuppe)

It could be argued that the German version of onion soup is superior to other versions you may have tried. Make this hearty, flavorful soup yourself, and see what you think!

Serves 4 | Prep. time 10 min. | Cooking time 40 min.

Ingredients
¼ cup butter
1 pound yellow onions, sliced
1 apple, peeled and sliced
2 tablespoons flour
4 cups beef stock
½ cup lager beer
1 teaspoon dried marjoram
Salt and pepper to taste
Slices of baguette, toasted, or croutons
5 tablespoons Emmental cheese, grated
¼ cup fresh chives, chopped

Directions
1. Melt the butter in a Dutch oven and add the onions. Cook until they are softened.
2. Add the apple and cook another few minutes.
3. Sprinkle on the flour and cook, stirring, for 2–3 minutes.
4. Add the beef stock, beer, marjoram, and salt and pepper. Simmer for about 20 minutes.
5. To serve, top the soup with croutons or slices of toasted baguette. Sprinkle with cheese and chives, and place the soup under the broiler until the cheese is melted and golden.

Milk Noodle Soup (Milchnudeln)

This pasta cooked in milk is the ultimate in comfort food. It's often served sweetened with honey and/or sugar, and we suggest you try it, even it sounds a little odd.

Serves 4 | Prep. time 10 min. | Cooking time 15 min.

Ingredients
4 ¼ cups whole milk
Pinch nutmeg
1 teaspoon salt
8 ounces pasta (small works best)
1 tablespoon honey (optional)
1 teaspoon sugar (optional)

Directions
1. In a Dutch oven or large pot, bring the milk to a boil and add the nutmeg and salt.
2. Add the pasta and reduce the heat. Simmer until the pasta is tender.
3. Serve hot. If it thickens too much you can choose to add more milk.
4. Serve with a drizzle of honey or a sprinkle of sugar, if desired.

German Beer and Cheddar Soup

We couldn't make a book on German foods and leave out the famous combination of beer and cheese! This soup cooks up in half an hour, and it even contains some hidden vegetables for nutrition. Serve it with a dense, flavorful bread.

Serves 4 | Prep. time 5 min. | Cooking time 25 min.

Ingredients
¼ cup butter
1 carrot, peeled and grated
1 apple, peeled and grated
1 large onion, diced
2 cloves garlic, crushed and minced
¼ cup all-purpose flour
1 ½ cups whole milk

16 ounces beer
1 tablespoon stone-ground mustard
½ cup heavy cream
10 ounces sharp cheddar, shredded (plus more for topping)
½ teaspoon salt
½ teaspoon black pepper
½ teaspoon red pepper flakes
⅛ teaspoon nutmeg
2 tablespoons fresh chives, for topping

Directions
1. In a Dutch oven or large pot, melt the butter. Add the carrot, apple, onion, and garlic, and cook for 10 minutes, stirring often.
2. Sprinkle on the flour. Cook and stir until the flour begins to darken, 2–3 minutes.
3. Gradually whisk in the milk until smooth. Add the beer and mustard and stir until it stops foaming.
4. Bring it to a boil, reduce the heat, and simmer until thickened.
5. Add the cream, cheese, salt, pepper, red pepper flakes, and nutmeg. Mix until everything is combined. Taste, and correct the seasonings if desired.
6. Serve hot with a topping of chives and extra cheese.

BREAD

Pretzels

You can't have a proper selection of German foods without the beloved pretzel. Crisp on the outside, deliciously moist and chewy inside, these are excellent with a beer and cheddar sauce or mustard.

Serves 24 | Prep. time 20 min. | Rest time 1 hour | Cooking time 20 min.

Ingredients
½ cup lukewarm water
1 ½ teaspoons sugar
1 tablespoon active dry yeast
¾ cup milk, lukewarm
4 teaspoons olive oil
1 teaspoon salt

1 cup whole wheat flour
2 ½ cups all-purpose flour, divided
¼ cup baking soda
Coarse salt for sprinkling

Directions
1. Line two large baking sheets with parchment paper.
2. In a large mixing bowl or the bowl of a stand mixer, combine the water, sugar, and yeast. Let it sit for 10 minutes to bloom.
3. Add the milk and oil.
4. Mix the salt into the whole wheat flour and add it to the bowl, together with 2 cups of the all-purpose flour. Mix until it is well combined, adding add more flour if it's needed to make the dough form a ball.
5. Cover and let the dough rise in a warm place for 45 minutes to an hour.
6. When the dough has almost finished rising, combine the baking soda with 2 quarts of water in a large pot. Bring it to a boil and keep it hot.
7. Preheat the oven to 425°F.
8. Split the dough in half and separate each half into 12 equal pieces.
9. Roll each piece into a rope about 16 inches long. Form circles with the ends overlapping, twist the ends, and fold the tips down to join with the circle. Repeat until all the pretzels are formed. Place them back on the sheets to rise for 10 more minutes.
10. In small batches, lower the pretzels into the simmering soda water and remove them when they rise to the top. Place them back on the sheets and sprinkle them with salt.
11. Bake for 15 minutes or until golden brown.

Bierocks

This delicious meat pocket is sure to become a household favorite. Make a large batch and keep them in the fridge for easy lunches and snacks.

Serves 8 | Prep. time 30 min. | Rest time 2¾ hours | Cooking time 25 min.

Ingredients
For the dough
1 cup milk, warm
¼ cup white sugar
1 tablespoon active dry yeast
4 cups all-purpose flour, divided
2 tablespoons butter, melted and cooled
1 egg, lightly beaten
1 teaspoon salt

For the filling
½ pound lean ground beef
1 small onion, diced
3 cups shredded cabbage
½ teaspoon garlic powder
¼ teaspoon salt
¼ teaspoon ground black pepper

2 tablespoons milk

Directions
1. Prepare the dough. In a large mixing bowl, dissolve the sugar in the warm milk. Sprinkle on the yeast and wait for it to bloom.
2. When the yeast is puffy and fragrant, add 2 cups of the flour and mix well.
3. Add the butter, egg, and salt and incorporate them into the mixture.
4. Add flour ¼ cup at a time until the dough is tacky but not sticky.
5. Knead on a lightly floured work surface for 10 minutes.
6. Lightly grease a clean bowl and add the dough, turning to coat it with oil. Cover it and let it rise in a warm place for an hour, or until it's doubled in bulk.
7. In the meantime, prepare the filling.
8. Place a large skillet over medium heat and brown the beef. Add the onion, cabbage, garlic powder, salt, and pepper.
9. Cook for 5–10 minutes, until the cabbage is tender.
10. Punch down the risen dough and divide it into 8 equal portions. Roll each out into a 4–5" circle.
11. Grease a baking sheet.
12. Spoon 2 generous tablespoons of filling into the center of each circle. Bring the edges up and pinch them, forming a ball around the filled center. Arrange the buns on the prepared baking sheet and let them rise for 30–45 minutes.

13. Preheat the oven to 375°F.
14. Brush the tops of the buns with milk and bake for 20–25 minutes, or until the tops are golden brown and the bottoms sound hollow when you tap them.

Pumpernickel Bread

What is served as pumpernickel in North America is not the same as the authentic German bread. In Germany, specifically Westphalia, this traditional bread contains very specific ingredients and is slowly baked into a dry, dense loaf.
Warning: this is a recipe for bread makers, as it requires some sourdough starter. Also, reserve this recipe for when you can devote the time required.

Makes 5 small or 2 large loaves | Prep. time 2 hours | Cooking time 15 hours (over a 3-day span)

Ingredients
7 ounces organic rye berries
3 tablespoons fed sourdough starter
12 ½ ounces organic dark rye flour
1 ½ cup lukewarm water

For the dough
12 ounces organic dark rye pumpernickel meal
12 ounces organic cracked rye
1 tablespoon salt
½ cup maple syrup
6 ounces dry-roasted sunflower seeds, unsalted
1 ½ cups lukewarm water, divided

Directions
1. In a saucepan, cover the rye berries with an inch of boiling water. Cover and leave them to soak overnight.
2. The same evening, combine the sourdough starter with the dark rye flour and lukewarm water. Cover the bowl and let it sit overnight in a warm place.
3. The next day, add water to the soaked rye berries until the ratio of water to berries is 3:1. Bring it to a boil, reduce the heat, and simmer for an hour or until the berries are tender. Keep watch, as you may need to add more water. Drain the berries and set them aside.
4. Grease 5 straight-sided canning jars (16 ounces) or two loaf pans.
5. In a large bowl or in a stand mixer, stir the pumpernickel meal, cracked rye, and salt.
6. Add the prepared sourdough mixture, syrup, sunflower seeds, and 1 ¼ cups of water.
7. Mix until the dough comes together, adding the remaining water if needed.
8. On a lightly floured surface, knead the dough. It should be elastic and tacky but not too sticky. Lightly

dust it with some rye flour. Cover and let it rise 30 minutes.
9. Knead the dough briefly to remove air bubbles and divide it evenly among your pans or jars, leaving an inch or two of headspace for them to rise.
10. Grease some squares of aluminum foil and fold them over the tops of the jars (or pans), greased side down. Let the bread rise in a warm place for 2–3 hours.
11. Preheat the oven to 300°F and move the rack to the bottom. Remove the foil and lightly spray the tops of the loaves with water, and then replace the foil as it was. Ensure the bread is covered tightly.
12. Place the jars or loaves in a large roasting pan or lidded casserole dish tall enough to hold them. Pour in an inch of hot water and place the cover on the pan.
13. Bake the loaves in the covered pan for an hour, and then reduce the heat to 210°F for 13 more hours, making sure to keep the water about an inch or two deep the whole time.
14. After 13 hours, turn the oven off but don't remove the pan.
15. After another hour has passed, place the baking pan on the counter and let everything cool. Keep the oven door closed.
16. After half an hour, gently remove the bread from the jars or loaf pans. Place them on the oven rack and close the door to let them dry for a few hours.
17. Remove the bread loaves from the oven. When they are completely cool, wrap them tightly. Wait until the next day to slice them.
18. The bread can be kept wrapped in the fridge for up to a month.

Potato Bread (Kartoffelbrot)

Potato bread is crunchy on the outside and moist on the inside, and it's easy to make. It's wonderful spread with butter as a snack, or as a side next to a bowl of steaming soup or stew,

Makes 1 loaf | Prep. Time 30 min. | Rest time 1 hour | Cooking time 50 min.

Ingredients
2 medium potatoes
¼ cup cooking water from the potatoes
1 teaspoon active dry yeast
1 tablespoon vegetable oil
2 ½ cups bread flour, plus more for kneading
1 teaspoon salt

Directions
1. Peel and chop the potatoes. Cover them with water (no salt) and simmer until they are tender.
2. Drain the potatoes well, reserving the water.
3. Mash the potatoes and set them aside.
4. Cool ¼ cup of the cooking liquid. When it's lukewarm, add the yeast and a teaspoon of the sugar and let it sit for 10 minutes to bloom.
5. In the bowl of a stand mixer, combine the proofed yeast with the potatoes, oil, flour, and salt. Mix with the paddle attachment first, and then switch to the dough hook. Knead for 10 more minutes.
6. Form the dough (it will be shaggy) into a ball and place it in a greased bowl. Cover and let it rise for half an hour.
7. Preheat the oven to 450°F and place the rack in the center.
8. Punch down the dough and form it into a ball. Line a bowl with a clean kitchen towel and place the dough in, seam down. Fold the towel over the dough and let it rise for half an hour.
9. Transfer the dough to a lightly greased baking sheet (side down for a smooth top, or seam up for a more rustic loaf). Bake for 45 to 50 minutes, and let it cool for half an hour before slicing.

Stollen

Stollen is a spiced fruit bread that is often served at Christmastime. It's thought to have originated in Dresden, where it's mentioned as far back as 1474. Make this loaf 2 weeks ahead of time so it can ripen

Makes 1 loaf | Prep. time 4 ½ hours | Rest time 2 weeks | Cooking time 45 min

Ingredients
½ cup dark raisins
½ cup sultana raisins
3 tablespoons candied lemon peel pieces
3 tablespoons candied orange peel pieces
2 ounces dark rum
½ cup warm milk
1 tablespoon yeast
⅓ cup sugar
4 cups all-purpose flour

1 egg
1 teaspoon vanilla extract
2 tablespoons lemon zest
¼ teaspoon salt
1 cup unsalted butter
⅔ cups all-purpose flour
¼ teaspoon ground nutmeg
¼ teaspoon ground cardamom
⅓ cup blanched almond pieces
½ cup butter (melted)
½ cup powdered sugar (for dusting)

Directions

1. Combine the raisins and candied peels in a medium mixing bowl and pour the rum over them. Mix well and let them sit overnight, stirring occasionally.
2. Combine the milk with the yeast and add a pinch of the sugar. Let it sit for 10 minutes to bloom.
3. In the bowl of a stand mixer, combine the remaining sugar with the 4 cups of flour, egg, vanilla, lemon zest, salt, and the yeast mixture. Using the dough hook, mix for 5–7 minutes. The dough will be shaggy and not ready to work with just yet. Set it aside.
4. Cream the butter and add the ⅔ cup of flour, together with the nutmeg and cardamom. Add this to the yeast dough and mix until it's smooth. Cover and let it rest for 30 minutes.
5. Turn the dough out onto a clean, floured surface and mix in the fruit and almonds. Let it sit for 20 minutes.
6. Roll the dough into a long rectangle and press the roller into the center of the shape to make an indent. Fold one side of the rectangle into the indent to make a stollen loaf.
7. Preheat the oven to 350°F and coat a stollen pan with butter. If you don't have a stollen pan you can use a baking sheet and fold a piece of foil to hold the sides of your loaf and prevent it from spreading too much.

8. Transfer the loaf to your pan and let it rise for 30 minutes. Brush the top with a little of the melted butter.
9. Bake for 35–45 minutes, until the loaf is golden. While it's still warm, brush it with the remaining butter and dust it liberally with icing sugar.
10. Once it's cooled, wrap it tightly in foil and store it in a cool place for 2–3 weeks to ripen.

Raisin Bread (Rosinenbrot)

Some German households still tend to make their own bread, and it's not hard to see why this pretty, light, and crispy loaf is a favorite.

Makes 1 loaf | Prep. time 30 min. | Rest time 1 hour 50 min. Cooking time 30 min.

Ingredients
1 cup milk
1 tablespoon active dry yeast
4 cups all-purpose flour
⅓ cup granulated sugar
1 teaspoon salt
¼ cup butter, melted
1 whole egg, lightly beaten
½ cup Sultana raisins
1 egg yolk, lightly beaten

Directions
1. In a saucepan, warm the milk (not too hot, or it will kill the yeast). Sprinkle the yeast on the milk and stir briefly to dissolve. Leave it for a few minutes to bloom.
2. In a large mixing bowl, combine the flour, sugar, and salt. Make a well in the center and add the milk mixture, butter, and egg.
3. With a wooden spoon, incorporate the dry ingredients into the wet until a dough forms.
4. Turn the dough out onto a clean, floured surface and knead for 10–15 minutes, until it is smooth and elastic.
5. Return the dough to the bowl, cover, and let it rise for an hour or until it has doubled in size.
6. Turn the dough out onto the counter again and add the raisins. Knead them in briefly.
7. Divide the dough into three equal parts and form three ropes, 16 inches long. Braid them together.
8. Prepare a baking pan with a sheet of parchment. Transfer the loaf to the pan and turn the ends under neatly. Cover and let it rise for 20 minutes.
9. Preheat the oven to 350°F.
10. Brush the loaf with egg yolk, and bake for 20–30 minutes, until it is golden brown.

DESSERTS

Black Forest Cake (Schwarzwälder Kirschtorte)

The Black Forest Region of Germany is famous for its beauty, its cuckoo clocks, its dense evergreen forests, and the Brothers Grimm fairy tales. There, newlywed couples traditionally plant a cherry tree, and from these, we get the delicious, rich Black Forest cake everyone loves.

Serves 8–12 | Prep. time 60 min. | Cooking time 30 min.

Ingredients
1 pound fresh cherries, pitted
¾ cup granulated sugar, divided
1 cup flour

¼ cup cocoa powder
½ teaspoon salt
4 eggs
1 teaspoon vanilla extract
1 tablespoon cornstarch
1 ¾ cups heavy cream
½ cup icing sugar
1 ounce kirsh or cherry brandy
2 ounces chocolate shavings
Candied cherries, to garnish

Directions
1. Preheat the oven to 350°F and butter an 8- or 9-inch high-sided cake pan.
2. Place the cherries in a saucepan with a few tablespoons of water and stir in ¼ cup of sugar. Cook them over low heat for about 15 minutes, and using a slotted spoon, remove the cherries to a separate bowl.
3. Sift the flour, cocoa, and salt together and set them aside.
4. Beat the eggs with the remaining ½ cup of sugar and the vanilla until they are light and frothy. Fold in the flour mixture and spread the batter in the cake pan.
5. Bake for 30 minutes, or until a toothpick inserted in the center comes out clean.
6. Meanwhile, heat the cherry liquid and add the cornstarch. Cook to thicken, and then pour it back over the cooked cherries. Let the mixture cool.
7. Beat the heavy cream with the cherry brandy and icing sugar until thick.
8. When the cake has baked and is cool, slice it into three equal discs. Arrange one disk on a cake plate.

9. Spread a layer of cherry compote and some whipped cream on the layer, and repeat for all three layers.
10. Use the remaining cream to frost the sides of the cake and cover with chocolate shavings. Garnish with the candied cherries.

Cinnamon Rolls (Franzbrötchen)

You often find these sweet little pastries in northern Germany, where they are often made with cinnamon, but sometimes with fruit or chocolate as well. They are like a cross between a cinnamon bun and a croissant.

Serves 12 | Prep. time 30 min. | Rest time 3 ½ hours | Cooking time 20–25 min.

Ingredients
1 cup whole milk, lukewarm
1 ½ teaspoons yeast
3 tablespoons granulated sugar, divided
4 ½ cups all-purpose flour, plus more for dusting
¾ teaspoon salt
2 eggs, at room temperature, lightly beaten
5 tablespoons unsalted butter, at room temperature
1 pound unsalted butter (in a single block), refrigerated
<u>For the filling</u>
¾ cup granulated sugar
2 teaspoons ground cinnamon

Directions
1. Place the warm milk in a bowl and stir in the yeast and a teaspoon of the sugar. Let it sit for 10 minutes to bloom.
2. Meanwhile, add the remaining sugar to the flour and mix in the salt.
3. Make a well in the center and add the eggs and 5 tablespoons of butter. Pour in the yeast mixture.
4. Stir and then knead the dough until it is smooth and elastic.
5. Place the dough in a clean, greased bowl, cover, and let it rise in a warm place for 2 hours.
6. When the dough has doubled in size, punch it down, knead briefly, and roll it into a 13-inch square.
7. Take the block of butter out of the fridge and dust it with flour. Roll it out into a 9-inch square, adding more flour as necessary.
8. Place the butter diagonally on your square of dough and fold the corners over it. Roll it out into a rectangle about 8x12 inches. Fold it into thirds (like a letter), cover, and refrigerate for 20 minutes.

9. Repeat the rolling, folding, and refrigerating two more times.
10. Preheat the oven to 400°F and grease or line a large baking sheet with parchment.
11. Combine the granulated sugar and cinnamon for the filling.
12. After the third time, you fold and chill the dough, cut it in half. Return one piece to the fridge and roll the other into a 13-inch square.
13. Sprinkle half the cinnamon sugar onto the dough, all the way from one edge to the other. Roll it up and cut it in 6 equal pieces.
14. Turn one of the pieces so the cut end is facing you. With the handle of a wooden spoon, gently press down across the center so the cut ends open and fan out a little, but don't cut all the way through.
15. Transfer the roll to the baking sheet and use your hands to arrange or fold in the ends a little toward the center, if necessary. Repeat for the remaining dough.
16. Cover the baking pan with a clean towel and let the rolls rise for 20 minutes.
17. Bake for 20–25 minutes, until the rolls are golden and laky and crisp on the bottom.

Vanilla Crescent Cookies (Vanillekipferl)

The dough for these cookies is delicate and just a little fussy, but the cookies are well worth the effort. Just keep it cold – remove only a portion from the fridge to work with at a time.

Serves 12 | Prep. time 10 min. | Chill time 1 hour | Cooking time 15 min.

Ingredients
2 cups all-purpose flour
Pinch salt
1 cup unsalted butter, room temperature, cubed
¾ cup icing sugar
¾ cup finely ground almonds, hazelnuts or walnuts
2 teaspoons vanilla extract

For coating
¾ cup powdered sugar

Directions
1. In a mixing bowl or the bowl of a stand mixer, combine all the ingredients. Mix for 2–3 minutes. If the dough does not come together, add a little water.
2. Press the dough into a ball and wrap it in plastic. Refrigerate for an hour.
3. Preheat the oven to 350°F and line two baking sheets with parchment paper.
4. Working with portions of the dough (keeping the unused portions refrigerated), roll out log shapes that are half an inch thick. Cut off 2-inch portions and pinch the ends to form crescents. Arrange the crescents on the baking sheets.
5. Repeat until all the dough is used.
6. Bake one sheet at a time for 12–15 minutes, or until the cookies feel firm but are not browned.
7. While they are still hot, sift the powdered sugar over them. Once they have cooled, give them a second coat.

Sunken Apple Cake
(Versunken Apfelkuchen)

This beautiful cake is simplicity itself to make, and the flavors of the butter and apple come through in this all-time favorite. Use a 9- or 10-inch springform pan to preserve the decorative top of the cake.

Serves 6 | Prep. time 20 min. | Cooking time 40 min.

Ingredients
2–3 apples, peeled, cored, and thinly sliced (Gala or Granny Smith work well)
1 tablespoon lemon juice
½ cup butter, room temperature
⅔ cup sugar
3 eggs
1 ¾ cups all-purpose flour
2 teaspoons baking powder

½ teaspoon salt
½ cup milk
2 teaspoons vanilla extract
1 tablespoon sugar
Powdered sugar for sprinkling

Directions
1. Preheat the oven to 350°F and butter a 9- or 10-inch springform cake pan.
2. Sprinkle the lemon juice over the apples and toss to coat.
3. Beat the butter with the sugar until the mixture is pale and light. One at a time, incorporate the eggs and beat until fluffy.
4. Sift in the flour, baking powder, and salt. Mix well.
5. Gradually add the milk and vanilla and mix until smooth. Pour the batter into the prepared cake pan.
6. Arrange the apples on top of the cake in a pattern of your choice, pressing them gently into the batter. Sprinkle with a tablespoon of sugar.
7. Bake for 35–40 minutes, or until the cake is golden and a toothpick inserted in the cake at the center comes out clean.
8. When the cake is cool, dust the top with powdered sugar.

German Gingerbread Cookies (Pfefferneusse)

This is a recipe that dates back to the middle ages. It's a kind of gingerbread cookie that is prepared with a glaze. They keep well for up to two weeks in an airtight container.

Makes 4 dozens | Prep. time 20 min. | Chill time 12 hours | Cooking time 55 min.

Ingredients
2 ¼ cups all-purpose flour
¼ cup almond meal
½ teaspoon baking soda
1 teaspoon ground cinnamon
½ teaspoon ground cloves
½ teaspoon ground ginger
¼ teaspoon ground allspice
⅛ teaspoon ground coriander
⅛ teaspoon ground mace

⅛ teaspoon ground nutmeg
¼ teaspoon salt
¼ teaspoon ground white pepper
½ cup packed brown sugar
¼ cup honey
⅓ cup butter
3 tablespoons heavy cream
1 large egg

For the glaze
2 ½ cups icing sugar
Up to ¼ cup hot water (use less water for a thicker glaze)

Directions
1. In a mixing bowl, combine the flour, almond meal, baking soda, and all the spices.
2. In a large saucepan, combine the brown sugar, honey, butter, and cream. Heat, stirring occasionally, until everything is dissolved and combined. Remove the pot from the heat and let it cool for 5–10 minutes.
3. Add the sugar liquid to the flour mixture, and stir in the egg. The dough will be sticky.
4. Wrap the dough tightly in plastic and refrigerate overnight, or for up to 2 days.
5. Preheat the oven to 350°F.
6. Divide the dough in half and roll it out into 2 strands just under an inch thick. Working quickly so the dough will be cold and easier to handle, cut off 1-inch pieces and roll them into balls. Arrange the balls on baking sheets.
7. Bake for 15 minutes or until the cookies are golden. Cool completely.
8. Measure the icing sugar into a medium bowl and add sufficient water to reach the consistency you like.
9. Using a fork, dip the cookies in the glaze and place them on a wire rack to set.

Bethmannchen Cookies

These Christmas cookies come from Frankfurt and are named for the Bethmann family. In the early 1900s, Theobald von Bethmann-Hollweg was the chancellor of the German Empire. The three almonds on the cookies are for his three sons.

Makes 30 cookies | Prep. time 15 min. | Cooking time 20 min.

Ingredients
½ cup icing sugar
¼ cup flour
1 egg, separated
8 ounces marzipan, coarsely grated
1 tablespoon milk
3 ounces blanched almond halves

Directions
1. Preheat the oven to 350°F and line a baking sheet with parchment paper.
2. Combine the icing sugar and the flour, and mix in the egg white and marzipan. Knead or mix until smooth.
3. Roll the dough into balls about the size of walnuts. If the dough is too sticky, add a little more flour. Keep your hands moist.
4. Combine the egg yolk with the milk and brush it onto the cookies. Arrange three almond halves on each cookie with the tips pointing up.
5. Bake for 15–20 minutes, until golden.

Plum Custard Cake
(Plum Kuchen)

We've made this recipe with a variety of fruits including raspberries, peaches, and of course, plums. Served warm, it's mouth-watering comfort food at its finest.

Serves 6 | Prep. time 15 min. | Cooking time 45 min.

Ingredients
1 cup all-purpose flour
2 tablespoons white sugar
1 teaspoon baking powder
½ cup cold butter, cubed
2 tablespoons heavy cream
1 egg, lightly beaten
1 teaspoon vanilla extract
2 ½ cups pitted and sliced plums
½ teaspoon cinnamon
¼ teaspoon ground ginger

For the custard
½ cup heavy cream
½ cup white sugar
1 egg
1 teaspoon vanilla extract

Directions
1. Preheat the oven to 350°F and butter an 8-inch springform cake pan.
2. In a mixing bowl, combine the flour, sugar, and baking powder. Cut in the butter until it is the texture of coarse meal.
3. Mix in the cream, egg, and vanilla extract and stir to combine.
4. Spread the dough in the prepared cake pan and pat it down.
5. Toss the plum slices with the spices and arrange them on the cake base. Bake for 20 minutes.
6. In a small bowl, whisk the custard ingredients together. Pour them over the cake and return it to the oven. Bake another 25 minutes, or until the custard is set.

Lemon Crullers
(Eberswalder Spritzkuchen)

These eggy treats come from a German town near the Polish border, and are traditionally served in the days just before the beginning of Lent, when the people would be using up their animal fats to save them from spoiling.

Serves 12–15 | Prep. time 20 min. | Cooking time 20 min.

Ingredients
For the crullers
1 ¼ cups water
¼ cup unsalted butter
1 cup all-purpose flour
¼ cup cornstarch
5 eggs
2 tablespoons sugar
½ teaspoon vanilla extract

1 teaspoon baking powder
Vegetable oil for deep frying

For the frosting
1 ½ cups icing sugar
Up to 2–3 tablespoons lemon juice

Directions
1. In a medium saucepan, boil the water and stir in the butter until melted.
2. Combine the flour and cornstarch and stir them into the water mixture until a dough forms. Return the pot to the burner and cook, stirring, another 2–3 minutes, until there is a white film on the bottom of the pot.
3. Move the dough to a mixing bowl and let it cool a little. One at a time, mix in the eggs. Add the sugar, vanilla, and baking powder and mix well.
4. Heat a few inches of oil in a heavy-bottomed pot.
5. Cut out 3–4 squares of parchment paper and spray them with cooking spray.
6. Transfer the dough to a piping bag with a wide star tip. Pipe circles onto the parchment.
7. When the oil is 365°F, carefully transfer the crullers into the oil by laying them in with the paper side up and then peeling away the paper. Don't crowd your pot, and cook the crullers until they are golden on both sides.
8. Remove them to a plate lined with paper towels. Make sure the oil is back up to temperature before you repeat the process with more dough.
9. Arrange a wire rack over a sheet of parchment. Combine the glaze ingredients in a bowl, adding just enough lemon juice to reach the consistency you like.
10. Dip the doughnuts into the glaze and place them on the rack to set.

Apple Strudel

Traditional strudel dough is made with only a few ingredients, and would have been hand stretched so thin it would cover a table. But you don't need to be an expert to give this a try – it will taste wonderful even if the dough is not paper thin.

Serves 6 | Prep. time 45 min. | Cooking time 50 min.

Ingredients
For the dough
¼ cup unsalted butter, melted
1 ½ cups all-purpose flour
Pinch of salt
⅓ cup water, lukewarm

For the apple filling
⅓ cup sultana raisins
2 tablespoons rum

3 large apples
1 tablespoon lemon juice
1 ½ teaspoons ground cinnamon
⅛ teaspoon nutmeg
½ cup granulated sugar
¼ teaspoon salt
¼ cup pecans, walnuts or almonds, finely chopped

To assemble
2 tablespoons all-purpose flour
6 tablespoons unsalted butter, melted
¼ cup breadcrumbs
¼ cup icing sugar

Directions
1. In a small bowl, combine the rum and raisins. Mix well and set them aside to soak.
2. Combine the ingredients for the dough and mix until a smooth dough forms.
3. Heat a medium saucepan under hot running water. Dry it well and line it with parchment. Place the dough in the pot, cover it, and let it sit for 30 minutes.
4. Meanwhile, peel and chop the apples. In a medium bowl, toss them with the lemon juice and season with the cinnamon, nutmeg, sugar, and salt. Drain the raisins and add them to the filling, together with the nuts.
5. Preheat the oven to 350°F and line a baking sheet with parchment paper.
6. On your worktop, lay out a clean, thin kitchen towel and sprinkle it with the flour. Roll the dough out as thin as you can on the towel.
7. Brush a little of the melted butter on the dough, and use your hands to spread the dough out until you have a rectangle about 12x18 inches (as thin as you can). Arrange the dough so the long side is in front of you.

8. Brush half the melted butter on the dough. Leaving a 6-inch strip on the right side and a 2-inch margin on the long edges, sprinkle the breadcrumbs along the center down the length of the dough.
9. Spread the apple filling on the breadcrumbs, but leave any juices in the bowl.
10. Fold the 2-inch edges over the filling. Starting from the short edge opposite the 6-inch margin, gently roll up the strudel using the towel to help.
11. Transfer the strudel to the prepared baking sheet and brush it with butter. Bake for about 50 minutes, brushing it twice more with butter while it bakes.
12. Sprinkle with icing sugar and serve warm.

Bee Sting Cake (Bienenstich)

This cake may be familiar to some, but the German version uses a brioche dough that sets it (in our opinion) above the standard cake type. It's worth the extra effort – and the pastry cream is out of this world.

Serves 12 | Prep. time 45 min. | Rising time 7 hours | Cooking time 25 min.

Ingredients

For the pastry cream
1 ¼ cups whole milk
3 large egg yolks
¼ cup sugar
¼ teaspoon salt
2 tablespoons all-purpose flour
2 tablespoons cornstarch
1 teaspoon pure vanilla extract or vanilla bean paste
2 teaspoons Grand Marnier Brandy, Kirsch, or Amaretto (optional)

Brioche dough
¼ cup whole milk
2 tablespoons honey
2 teaspoons active dry yeast
2 large eggs, lightly beaten
¾ cup all-purpose flour
2 tablespoons sugar
½ teaspoon salt
1 cup plus 2 tablespoons bread flour, divided
½ cup unsalted butter, softened

For the topping
¼ cup unsalted butter (4 tablespoons)
¼ cup sugar
¼ cup honey
Pinch of salt
¾ cup slivered almonds

Directions
1. Prepare the pastry cream. In a medium saucepan, heat the milk just to the boiling point.
2. In a heatproof bowl, mix the egg yolks with the sugar. Sift in the flour and cornstarch and mix well.

3. Slowly add the hot milk, whisking briskly to prevent the yolk from curdling.
4. Pour the mixture into a clean saucepan and cook until it boils, whisking constantly. Let it boil for one minute and then remove it from the heat.
5. Add the vanilla and the liqueur, if using.
6. Pour the cream into a clean jar, cover, and let it cool. Refrigerate for up to 2 days. (Mix before using)
7. Prepare the brioche dough. Heat the milk and honey until lukewarm, and add the yeast. Let it sit for 10 minutes to bloom.
8. Warm the bowl of a stand mixer and slowly add the eggs, all-purpose flour, sugar, and salt. Mix on low speed until well combined.
9. With the mixer running, gradually add the bread flour just until the dough comes away from the sides of the bowl.
10. Slowly incorporate the butter.
11. Turn the dough out onto a lightly floured counter and knead to ensure everything is well combined. Form it into a ball and place it in a greased bowl. Cover and let it rise for 2 hours, until it has doubled in size.
12. After it has risen, punch it down, knead briefly, and return it to the bowl to rise for at least another 4 hours (and up to 12) until it has doubled in size again.
13. Grease a 9-inch springform pan. Reshape the dough to make a smooth ball and gently arrange it in the pan, pressing down slightly. Cover and let it rise for an hour.
14. Preheat the oven to 350°F.
15. Make the topping. In a saucepan over medium heat, mix the butter, sugar, honey, and salt. Bring it to a low boil.
16. Remove the pot from the heat and add the almonds. Mix well, and pour it over the cake. Bake

for 20–25 minutes, until the topping is golden and bubbly.
17. Let it cool for 10 minutes before removing the springform pan. Let it cool completely.
18. To assemble the cake, carefully cut it in half using a sharp serrated knife. Spread the cream on the bottom half and place the top on.

RECIPE INDEX

BEEF DISHES — 5
- Beef Rouladen — 5
- Sauerbraten — 7
- False Hare (Falscher Hase) — 9
- Meat Patties (Frikadellen) — 11
- German Gulasch — 13
- Cabbage Rolls with Gravy (Kohlrouladen) — 15

PORK DISHES — 17
- Pork Schnitzel — 17
- Bratwurst — 19
- Currywurst — 21
- Maultaschen — 23
- Bratwurst Supper — 25

CHICKEN DISHES — 27
- German Chicken Fricassee — 27
- Oktoberfest Roast Chicken (Weisn Hendle) — 29
- Beer Grilled Chicken — 31
- Drunken Chicken in Red Wine (Beschwipster Huhn) — 33
- Black Forest Chicken Cordon Bleu — 35

SEAFOOD DISHES — 37
- Fish Burgers (Fischbrötchen) — 37
- Cod in Mustard Cream Sauce — 39
- German Beer Fish (Bier Fisch) — 41
- Marinated Fried Herring — 41

SIDE DISHES — 45
- Traditional German Potato Salad — 45
- Spaetzle — 47
- Sauerkraut — 49
- Potato Pancakes (Kartoffelpuffer) — 51
- Potato Dumplings (Kartoffelkloesse) — 53
- Onion Pie (Zwiebelkuchen) — 55
- Red Cabbage — 57
- German Pancake (Pfannkuchen) — 59

SOUPS   **61**
   Oxtail Soup   61
   Midnight Soup (Mitternachtssuppe)   63
   Lentil and Pork Shank Stew   65
   Onion Soup (Zwiebelsuppe)   67
   Milk Noodle Soup (Milchnudeln)   69
   German Beer and Cheddar Soup   71

BREADS   **73**
   Pretzels   73
   Bierocks   75
   Pumpernickel Bread   77
   Potato Bread (Kartoffelbrot)   81
   Stollen   83
   Raisin Bread (Rosinenbrot)   85

DESSERTS   **87**
   Black Forest Cake (Schwarzwälder Kirschtorte)   87
   Cinnamon Rolls (Franzbrötchen)   89
   Vanilla Crescent Cookies (Vanillekipferl)   93
   Sunken Apple Cake (Versunken Apfelkuchen)   95
   German Gingerbread Cookies (Pfefferneusse)   97
   Apple Strudel   105
   Bethmannchen Cookies   99
   Plum Custard Cake (Plum Kuchen)   101
   Lemon Crullers (Eberswalder Spritzkuchen)   103
   Bee Sting Cake (Bienenstich)   105

APPENDIX

Cooking Conversion Charts

1. Measuring Equivalent Chart

Type	Imperial	Imperial	Metric
Weight	1 dry ounce		28 g
	1 pound	16 dry ounces	0.45 kg
Volume	1 teaspoon		5 ml
	1 dessert spoon	2 teaspoons	10 ml
	1 tablespoon	3 teaspoons	15 ml
	1 Australian tablespoon	4 teaspoons	20 ml
	1 fluid ounce	2 tablespoons	30 ml
	1 cup	16 tablespoons	240 ml
	1 cup	8 fluid ounces	240 ml
	1 pint	2 cups	470 ml
	1 quart	2 pints	0.95 l
	1 gallon	4 quarts	3.8 l
Length	1 inch		2.54 cm

* Numbers are rounded to the closest equivalent

2. Oven Temperature Equivalent Chart

Fahrenheit (°F)	Celsius (°C)	Gas Mark
220	100	
225	110	1/4
250	120	1/2
275	140	1
300	150	2
325	160	3
350	180	4
375	190	5
400	200	6
425	220	7
450	230	8
475	250	9
500	260	

* Celsius (°C) = T (°F)-32] * 5/9
** Fahrenheit (°F) = T (°C) * 9/5 + 32
*** Numbers are rounded to the closest equivalent

Printed in Germany
by Amazon Distribution
GmbH, Leipzig